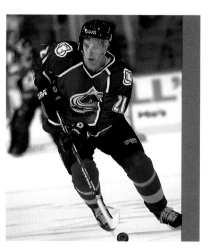
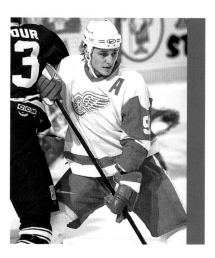

Hockey
THE NHL WAY

The Basics

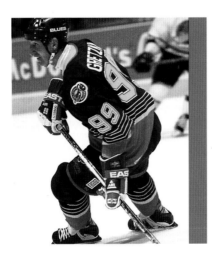

Sean Rossiter

Foreword by
Pat Quinn

GREYSTONE BOOKS

Douglas & McIntyre

Vancouver/Toronto

For the late Father David Bauer, the father of scientific coaching in Canada, the game's great missionary, and the patron saint of hockey in its purest form.

Copyright © 1996 by Sean Rossiter

97 98 99 00   5 4 3

Greystone Books
A division of Douglas & McIntyre Ltd.
1615 Venables Street
Vancouver, British Columbia
Canada V5L 2H1

Canadian Cataloguing in Publication Data
Rossiter, Sean, 1946 –
    The basics
    (Hockey the NHL way)

    ISBN 1-55054-499-3

    1. Hockey. I. Title. II. Series
GV847.R67 1996   796.962'2   C96-910234-8

Editing by Anne Rose and Kerry Banks
Cover and text design by Peter Cocking
Front cover photograph: *Mark Messier* by Bruce Bennett/Bruce Bennett Studios
Back cover photographs: *Pavel Bure* by Kent Kallberg Studios
    All other photos by Bruce Bennett Studios. Photographers:
    Paul Kariya: Art Foxall • *Peter Forsberg, Wayne Gretzky:* Bruce Bennett •
    Sergei Fedorov: Mark Hicks • *Ed Belfour:* Claus Andersen
Printed and bound in Canada by Friesens
Printed on acid-free paper

The publisher gratefully acknowledges the assistance of the Canada Council and of the British Columbia Ministry of Tourism, Small Business and Culture.

Contents

Our players

Jordan Sengara   Daniel Birch   Will Harvey   Tyler Dietrich

Michelle Marsz   Rob Tokawa   Brandon Hart   Kendall Trout

Jesse Birch   Nicolas Fung

Special thanks

Special thanks to the University of British Columbia Thunderbird Winter Sports Centre and general manager Rick Noonan, and to the staff of Cyclone Taylor Sports: Rick and Mark Taylor, and Mike Cox. Todd Ewen of the Mighty Ducks of Anaheim came through for this book in overtime. Thanks, as well, to the dedicated parents of the *Hockey The NHL Way* All-Stars, who always rise to the occasion. Finally, many thanks to Norm Jewison, Devin Smith and Veronica Varhaug of the Vancouver Canucks.

Our coaching advisory staff

Pat Quinn
President, general manager and coach, the Vancouver Canucks

Two-time winner of the Jack Adams Trophy as Coach of the Year in the National Hockey League, Pat Quinn has coached three NHL clubs. His Philadelphia Flyers set an NHL record with their 35-game undefeated streak in 1979–80. Quinn played more than 600 games as a hard-rock NHL defenseman over nine years.

Ron Smith
Head coach, Cincinnati Cyclones

A former head coach of the New York Rangers, Ron Smith is considered one of the brightest minds in the game. As technical director for the Ontario Hockey Association, he was instrumental in creating the Canadian national coaching certification program. He has coached at every level.

Paul Carson
Coaching coordinator, the British Columbia Amateur Hockey Association

An assistant coach of the UBC Thunderbirds since 1992, Paul Carson also supervises his community's minor hockey skill development program. He is a special education teacher working in the field of technology for students with special needs.

Jack Cummings
Hockey coordinator, the Hollyburn Country Club

Jack Cummings played goal for four years at both the Junior A level and with the University of Alberta. He was an assistant coach to the U of A's legendary Clare Drake for six years, and has been hockey coordinator at the Hollyburn Country Club in West Vancouver for four years.

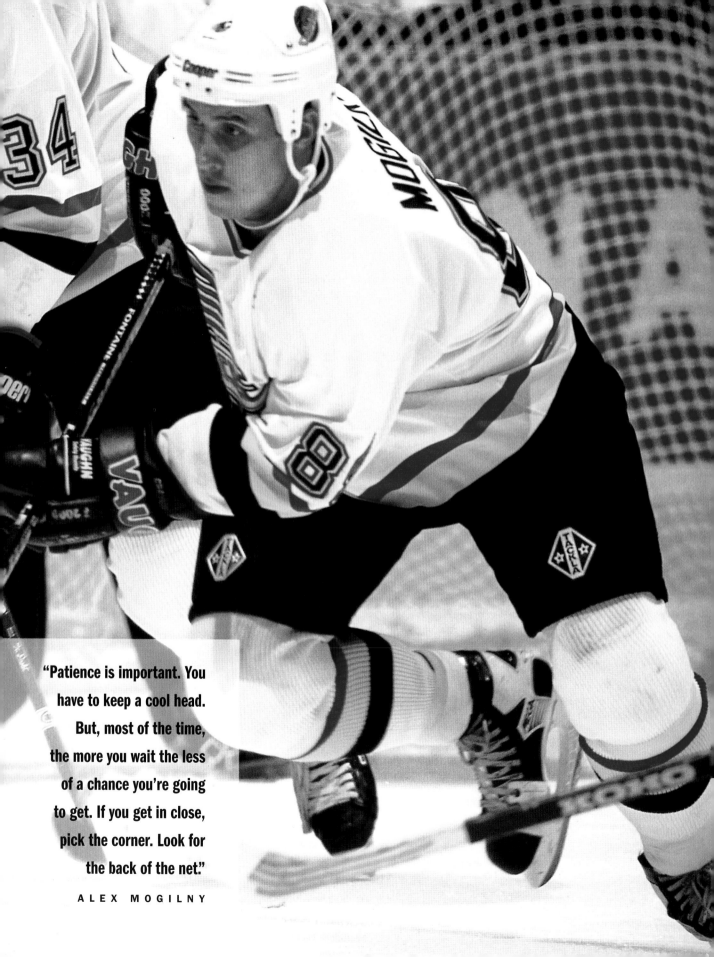

"Patience is important. You have to keep a cool head. But, most of the time, the more you wait the less of a chance you're going to get. If you get in close, pick the corner. Look for the back of the net."

ALEX MOGILNY

Foreword

Hockey the NHL Way: The Basics teaches the skills any player from age 8 to 12 needs for a solid start in the world's fastest and most colourful sport. Seeing young NHL greats such as Pavel Bure, Pat LaFontaine, Scott Niedermayer and Patrick Roy perform the skills this book teaches will inspire young students of the game.

I like to see young people who are learning hockey try different positions so they can better understand all aspects of the game. This book teaches the skills needed to play any position. And the basics of fair play and sportsmanship are an important part of learning the game.

The great game of hockey is more than just the elite players of the NHL. It's kids waking up early for practice, it's parents who get involved, and it's coaches who give of their time and experience to help young people learn. Hockey means teamwork, dedication and friendships to remember—no matter how far you go in the game.

Pat Quinn
The Vancouver Canucks

Introduction

Often the first things new fans like about hockey are the loud parts—bodies hitting the boards, pucks hitting the glass.

As a player, you know better. Hockey is the wind in your face, the rasp of your skates on the ice, the click of a pass on your stick, the joy of making a big save. At its best, hockey is a game of non-stop action that requires every player to master difficult skills *and* perform two or more of them at once.

Hockey is as tough and physical a game as there is: the ice and boards are hard, and the sticks, skates and pucks with which it is played can be dangerous if not handled carefully. As a player, you have an obligation to make the game as safe as possible for everyone on the rink. That means keeping your stick down and your temper under control. It also means treating referees and linesmen—and their decisions—with respect. Like other demanding sports, hockey can bring out the best and worst in people.

Yet, of all the team sports, hockey is the one where players usually line up to shake hands after an important game. It is an international sport that has led to understanding among people who once had only cold weather in common. Sportsmanship is what makes this great game a thing of beauty.

Most important, never demean your opponents. They are not your enemy. Honour your opponents, without whom you have no game. Think about it. The better they are, the better the game will be. Play to win, play hard and play clean. By giving the game your best, you honour your opponents. By honouring your opponents, you honour yourself.

One of the greatest scorers ever to play the game, Mario Lemieux seems to think up new ways to put the puck in the net each time he plays.

If you can't skate, you can't play hockey. The main difference between players who rise to the highest levels of the game and those who don't is skating.

For many years, coaches believed there were good skaters and bad skaters, and that there was no way to improve the bad ones. Yet figure skaters are often faster than hockey players. That is because figure skaters work for hours, every day, on a single aspect of hockey—skating under control. No wonder figure skaters have found an important place at hockey schools. Hockey players can learn a lot from them about the most important skill in the game.

S K A

TINC

The first steps

Quickness is more important than sheer speed in hockey. The first few steps you take usually determine who gets to loose pucks first. Those first few steps should be short, driving, explosive steps, like a sprinter leaving the starting blocks.

- Have your feet close together, toes out.
- Dig the toes of your blades into the ice, lean forward, and drive. Keep your upper body relaxed. Driving your arms forward can add power to a quick start.
- Make a habit of always getting off to a quick start.
- After your first few strides, begin to lengthen your stride.
- Push off hard on each stride so your blades make a rasp sound.

Lengthening your stride

The longer your stride, the less energy you need to get where you're going. Lean forward from the waist. Extend each stride as far backward as possible. At the end of your power stroke, your

Getting started

Will has his heels close together, toes out, weight leaning forward.

He starts off with short, choppy steps, driving off the forward inside edge.

After five or six chops, he lengthens his stride, pushing off his stride leg.

back foot should be as square as possible to the direction you're moving in. A final toe flick completes the stroke.

Concentrate on extending each stride as far as possible. Meanwhile, bend the front leg—the glide leg—to keep your body low to the ice. By bending the glide leg, you give it a more powerful thrust when it becomes the stride leg.

Crossovers

Use crossovers to add power and speed as you turn. You can begin practising crossovers by walking on the ice, following one of the faceoff circles. Simply lift your outside skate over the inside one, and transfer your weight to the new inside skate.

Skating backward

Skating backward is easier than most people think. Just so you can feel better about trying it, start next to the boards. Grab the boards if you feel yourself falling.

Start skating backward by swinging one hip out and making a C-shaped arch behind you with the skate on that side. Glide with the other foot. Make another C-arch with the skate you used the last time. Now do the same with the other skate.

Try to generate power by thrusting hard against the front inside edge of the skate you are cutting C-shaped arches with. Now alternate C-arches, one foot after the other.

T I P

As you try crossing over while gliding, remember to lean forward and into the turn for balance.

Jordan swings his left hip and begins a C-cut with his left skate.

He finishes the C-cut and is already shifting weight to his right leg.

He is about to begin the right-side C-cut and is moving backward, under control.

Skate better

Skating tips

- Keep low to the ice. Thrust hard with your back leg.
- Your upper leg muscles should feel the strain. That's where power comes from.
- When speed is what you want, carry your stick with your top hand alone.

As fast as any player in the NHL, Paul Coffey makes sure his skates are just the way he wants them. His speed allows him to play at both ends of the ice.

Pulling the cart

Pull a teammate with both of you holding a stick and driving hard down the ice. The teammate can provide more or less resistance by turning the toes of his or her skates in, or by keeping them parallel.

Figure-8s

To work on crossovers in both directions, skate from centre ice toward one corner, around behind the net, back to centre and toward the corner opposite the one you started from. Continue around the net, back to centre ice, and repeat.

Stops & starts

No player enjoys doing stops and starts. Here's why you should do them.

The Russians were the first to make hockey coaching a science. A coach of the famous Central Red Army club once figured out how many stops the average player makes during a game. The total was between 150 and 200! A player who works as hard as he should makes seven to 10 stops during each shift. And for almost every stop there is a start.

There's no secret to doing stops and starts. Just do more of them in practice. And make every one a quick start.

Skating drills

When we imagine playing in the National Hockey League, we dream of scoring the Stanley Cup-winning goal, usually in overtime. Few of us dream of making big saves in overtime, and even fewer imagine ourselves preventing the Cup-winning goal with a timely backcheck. Yet we all know there is more to hockey than just scoring goals.

But goals are what highlight tapes are made of, and scoring more of them than your opponents wins the game. Goals are simply the result of doing many other things right. Those other things—controlling the puck, passing and receiving the puck, shooting, and winning faceoffs—are what this chapter of *Hockey the NHL Way: The Basics* is all about.

OFF

PETER FORSBERG ▶

The most important skill in hockey, after skating, is puck control.

To be an effective player, whether forward or defense, you have to be able to carry the puck and defend it from checkers, and be able to give and receive passes. These skills must be mastered so well that you don't need to look at the puck on your stick or think about what to do with it.

NHL players work on their sticks. You should do the same. Try a shorter stick, as Wendel Clark did, for better puck control. Or try one with a straighter blade to improve your backhand moves. Some players even shorten the blades of their sticks for a better feel. Give these ideas a try. Your stick should be a part of you. It deserves your time and care.

Your stick is not the only puck-handling tool you have. You are allowed to catch a flying puck as long as you drop it right away. And your skateblades are almost as important as your stick in controlling the puck. Learn to use your skates to control the puck:

- along the boards,
- by taking passes at your feet and
- by kicking the puck up to your stickblade.

PUCK CONTROL

Known best for his mean streak, Mark Messier does the little things well: faceoffs, backhand shots, shooting off the back foot, penalty killing.

Pierre Turgeon seldom looks at the puck but always controls it. Here he protects the puck by keeping the checker away with his body.

The secret to puck control is in your hands. Grip your stick lightly. Learn to cup the puck with your stickblade—that is, lean the stickblade over the puck. And carry the puck positioned in the middle of your stickblade.

Most of the time, keep your hands 8–12 inches/20–30 cm apart, at the top of the stick. Use your bottom hand to grip mostly with your fingers, not your palm. Don't squeeze the stick. Good puck handlers know that when they are being checked, it's a good idea to shorten their grip (by moving both hands down the shaft) to get closer to the puck.

Like so much in hockey, good puck control is a result of doing other things right. Being able to stop on a dime and then sprint away is a skating skill that can help you keep the puck. Handling the puck with your skates allows you to keep control when your

Jordan shows the proper grip for puck control.

Your skates can be as useful as your stick for puck control . . .

. . . when you use them to move the puck from behind you up to your stick.

Puck control secrets

stick is being checked or held. Seeing the play and knowing where the puck will be is a puck-control skill. How well do you see around you on the ice? Do you look over both shoulders when you skate into corners for the puck? Do you chase the puck, or do you know where it's going so that you can get there first? And do you know what you are going to do with the puck before you get it?

No single skill stands alone in hockey. It takes many skills working together for you to control the puck.

Stop & go

One way to beat a checker is to quickly cup the puck with your stickblade, and, when the checker stops, start again. When you stop, let your momentum bend your knees and bring you into a crouch. This is a good position from which to start again.

Pass to yourself

If you are anywhere near the boards and a defender is in your path, shoot the puck at the boards. Then skate around the defender and pick up the pass. The puck will rebound at the same angle as you shot it.

Puck control tricks

Protect the puck by keeping your body between the puck and the checker.

Remember: a pass to yourself off the boards rebounds at the same angle you shot it.

Use your body to protect the puck

When a checker is close, always try to keep your body between the checker and the puck. Be aware of the checker's stick, and move your opponent's stick out of the way to protect the puck from it.

In the offensive zone, look for open ice

Just keeping control of the puck will lead to scoring chances when you are near your opponent's net. Don't throw the puck away. Find open ice and move into it. As checkers come to you, your teammates will be open for passes.

Czech flash Jaromir Jagr bursts between two defensemen. His reach means he can control the puck far away from himself, in any direction.

Slalom drill

Put cones or pieces of equipment in a line, 6 or 7 feet/1.8 or 2.1 m apart. Stickhandle past the left side of the first cone, then past the right side of the next. This zigzagging forces you to stickhandle on the right and left sides of your body. Concentrate on form. Cup the puck. Feel it through your hands.

Against the grain

First, pick one player to be the "coach." Everyone then skates around the rink, in the same direction, with a puck. As the "coach" calls their names, two or three players begin stick-handling in the opposite direction. This forces them to keep their heads up to avoid other players.

Keepaway

The next three puck-control drills are forms of Keepaway. Because these drills are intense, they should be kept short. It is also important to avoid mismatches.

Circle drill: Two players, one puck. Both players must stay inside the faceoff circle. You'll know who's winning. Knocking the puck outside the circle results in the other player taking possession.

Pylon drill: Two pylons, 10 feet/3 m apart. Two skaters and a puck in-between. Score by playing the puck against your opponent's pylon. No shooting.

Five puck Keepaway: First, decide who will be the "coach." Then the rest of the players start skating with five pucks. Everybody tries to keep possession of a puck. The five players with a puck when the "coach" yells stop are the winners. There will be everything from one-on-one to four-on-one battles, so limit this drill to two or three minutes. No body checking.

Puck control drills

There is an old saying in hockey that the puck moves faster than any player can skate. It is also said that a team that passes well is making the puck do the work. Both sayings are true. Opponents who can pass well make you skate hard the entire game—just chasing the puck.

Passing is the skill that makes you more than an individual player. When you pass the puck, you become part of a team. The most basic team skill, passing requires two people: a passer and a receiver. Receiving a pass is often more difficult than giving one. Practise both aspects. You will see a lot more of the puck if your teammates know you are a dependable pass receiver.

Always remember that when you have the puck, you have at least four options—four teammates you can pass to. Passing is one way to maintain puck control among the five skaters on the ice.

Passing is a skill you can easily work on and soon improve at. Most young players don't practise it enough. Yet if you are a good passer, you can become one of the top players in your age group. Wayne Gretzky's passing skills have made him the highest scorer in hockey history.

PASSING

James Norris and Conn Smythe Trophy winner Brian Leetch is one of hockey's best passers. Here he uses both hands to move the puck out of his zone.

There are four basic passes in hockey. In each case, make sure that you:

- keep both hands away from your body, so that the stickblade stays square to the target until the follow-through, and
- cup the puck with your stickblade.

If you find your top hand is tight against your body, your stick may be too long or the lie may be incorrect.

The forehand pass

This is the easiest pass to make: a simple sweep of the stick toward the target. If your receiver is moving, remember to aim the puck well ahead of the receiver's stick, not their body. Bring the puck back to your back foot, release at the front foot. Follow through low, pointing your stickblade at the target.

Making passes

Jesse has his eye on his teammate, his stick cupping the puck . . . and his top hand away from his body. His hands work as a unit.

He follows through, shifting his weight and pointing his stick at the target.

The backhand pass

This pass is used when you want to get the puck to someone on your backhand side. Sight your target out of the corner of your eye. Try to keep your lower shoulder down, so your stickblade—and the puck—stay on the ice. Again, hands move together. The motion of a backhand pass causes your upper body to twist and your lower shoulder and hand to rise, making it easier to raise the puck. Follow through low. Stickblade square to the target.

The flip pass

To avoid sticks or bodies on the ice between you and your receiver, use a flip pass. Use your wrists to draw the puck toward yourself, and snap your stickblade up and under the puck. But don't overdo it. This is a pass, not a shot. Remember, the puck must land flat on the ice before it reaches the target.

The drop pass

This is the quickest way to move the puck between teammates, and often results in an unchecked puck carrier. The passer simply stops the puck and leaves it for the trailing teammate. But beware. Make sure that the player behind you is your teammate. If it isn't, your opponents are off on a breakaway—and you are going in the wrong direction.

Upper hand away from the body, front shoulder down. Cup the puck.

Smooth follow-through. Weight on the front foot, point the stick at the target. Look where the pass is going.

Making passes

Passing checklist

- The right pass is usually the easy pass. The longer the pass, the less likely it will get there.
- Hands work together, not against each other. Keep your stickblade square to the target.
- If you are the puck carrier, try to make eye contact with your receiver. Many passes go untouched because the receiver has no idea they are coming.

A pass that is not received loses your team the puck most of the time. Count the number of passes tried, but not received, the next time you watch a game. Even in the NHL, too many players give up on passes that are not perfect.

Receiving passes is more difficult than making them. Practise receiving bad passes. Passes behind you, passes into your skates, passes coming from behind, passes that arrive in the air—all are chances to show how much you want the puck.

If the pass is off-target: Reach for the pass by dropping your bottom hand off your stick. This will extend your reach. Just stop the puck with your stick held by your top hand, then go after it.

If the pass is behind you: There are two things you can do. You can stop. Or you can reach back with your top hand on the stick and your stickblade angled so the puck will rebound up to your back skate. Kick the puck up to your stick, which you are now holding with both hands.

Receiving passes

Bad pass. Will lets go of the stick with his bottom hand and reaches with the top hand only. Front knee bends deep to give him better reach.

The puck will deflect ahead off Will's back skateblade to his stick.

T I P

To improve your pass receiving, get your elbows up as the puck gets close. This helps you get your entire stickblade on the ice.

If the pass is into your skates: Angle your skate on the side the pass is coming from, toe in, and deflect the puck up to your stick. Or, if the pass is coming further back, put one foot behind the other, creating a 2-foot/61-cm-long target for the puck to hit. Shorten up on your stick to control the puck better when it arrives.

If the pass is off the ice: Try to catch the pass without closing your hand on the puck. Just stop the puck with your open palm, drop it in front of you, and play the puck with both hands on your stick. Don't wave your stick at high passes.

Pass receiving checklist

- The trick to receiving passes is to be available. When your team has the puck, look for open ice.
- Think "catching," not "stopping," the puck when you receive a pass. Relax your grip. Reach toward the puck and absorb its impact.
- Part of being available for a pass is making it easy for the passer. Be visible. Try to skate across the passer's field of vision in the neutral zone. Hold your stick on the ice as a target.
- Sometimes the long way around is the shortest route to receiving the puck. By skating in a semicircle to a spot not

> ### N H L   T I P
> "The key to receiving a bad pass is to use your entire body. Practise taking pucks off your skates and using your stick to knock down passes in the air."
> **P A U L   K A R I Y A**

Jordan reaches back for a pass behind him. His stick deflects the puck toward him . . .

. . . and he kicks it up with his back foot . . .

. . . to his stickblade, angled inward to receive the puck. This requires practise.

Receiving passes

far away, you can be at full speed when the puck comes, and be better able to see it coming.
- Receive a bouncing puck with your skate behind your stick-blade. Don't lift your stick off the ice. Back it up with your foot.
- Don't give up on bad passes. The more often you convert bad passes to completed passes, the more you'll get the puck.

Here Joe Sakic reaches for a bad pass. Turn broken plays into goals. Making the effort on bad passes means you'll get the puck more.

Most of the team drills in hockey involve passing. Here are a few simple drills that focus on this skill alone.

Playing catch

Two players face each other, 10–15 feet/3–4.5 m apart. Concentrate on keeping your hands and elbows away from your body. Make smooth, accurate passes, and follow through with your stickblade square to the target. Release the puck off the toe of the stick in a heel-to-toe action. The receiver reaches a few inches/centimetres toward the incoming pass. Lay a stick between the two players and practise flip passes.

Circle drill

Five or six players stand around the rim of a circle. Put your sticks on the ice and to the side as targets. The idea is to make smooth, accurate passes that hit the receiver's stick.

Pig-in-a-poke

Same as above, with one player, or "pig," in the middle trying to intercept. With skilled passers, add another "pig," then another puck. Players who have their passes intercepted or deflected move into the middle.

Skating & passing

Two players skate side-by-side, passing back and forth. The receiver stickhandles once or twice before returning the pass. Concentrate on leading the receiver with each pass.

Passing drills

The fun part of hockey is shooting. After all, scoring goals is the whole idea of the game. But being a hard shooter does not make you a goal scorer.

Brett Hull says it is more important to shoot quickly, and get your shot on the net, than it is to shoot hard. Joe Sakic knows that you can often catch a goalie off-guard by shooting sooner than expected.

Most young players want to develop a hard shot. But a hard shot makes nothing but noise if it misses the net. Work on accuracy first. You can practise shooting both on and off the ice. Always shoot for a specific spot. Then, once you can hit that spot often, work on getting the shot away quickly. Try shooting off both feet, and in mid-stride.

A hard shot will come in time, as you grow. For now, an accurate shot will always give you a chance to score. And a quick shot will put the puck in the net. There are three stages to any good shot. It's like shooting a gun. Think:

- I sight the target
- I load the gun—get the puck in a position of power
- Pull the trigger

SHOOTING

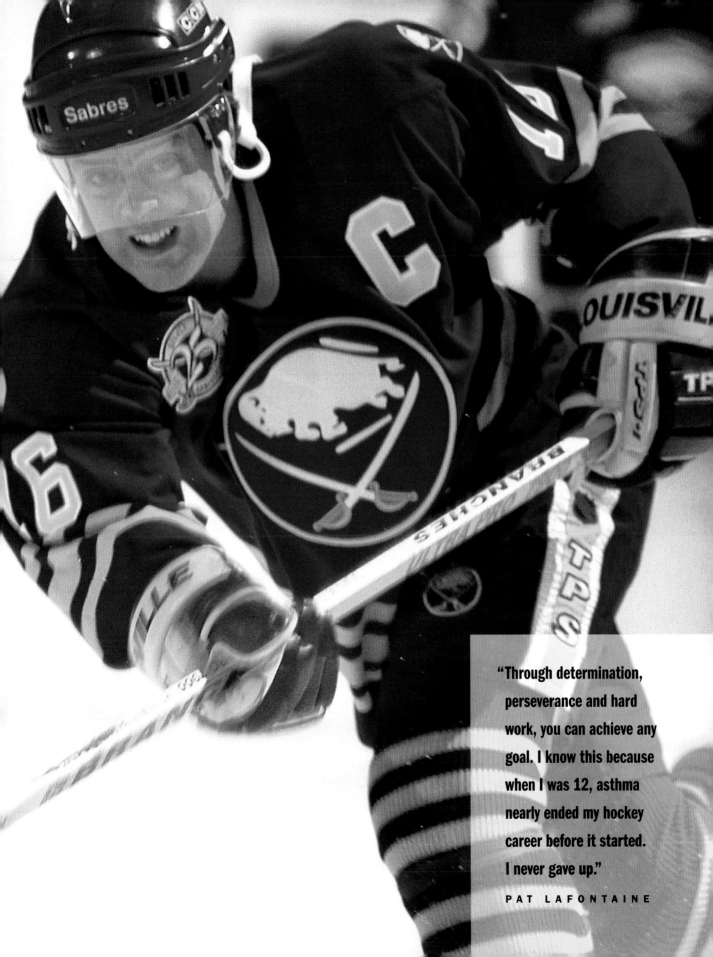

"Through determination, perseverance and hard work, you can achieve any goal. I know this because when I was 12, asthma nearly ended my hockey career before it started. I never gave up."

PAT LAFONTAINE

The wrist shot is an all-purpose, hard, accurate shot. It can be used when you are standing still or skating fast.

How to do it

Body position: Try to stay relaxed. Cup the puck with the middle of your stickblade. Feel it there. Keep your eyes on the target.
The shot: Sweep your stick forward. Just as it passes your body, bend both wrists back. Then snap them closed. The upper wrist pulls back on the top of your stick. The lower wrist supplies power and determines how high the shot will go.
Follow-through: Shift your weight to your front skate and follow through, aiming your stickblade at the target. To keep your shot low, follow through with your lower wrist on top of your stick and the toe of your stick pointing at your target.

The wrist shot

A textbook wrist shot starts with the puck well back . . .

. . . Jesse's power stroke is bending his stick as he lets the shot go . . .

. . . and follows through, pointing his stickblade at the target and rolling his bottom wrist over.

Wrist shot checklist

- Use both wrists. Turn both wrists open, and snap both closed at the moment of release. Feel your upper thumb pull the top of your stick toward your body.
- Shift weight from your back to front skate for power.
- Turn your body into the shot.
- Follow through, pointing your stickblade at your target, at the height you want. Feel your lower thumb curl around your stick to keep the shot low.

The closest thing to a secret weapon in hockey is the backhand shot. Vincent Damphousse uses it. Adam Oates uses a straight, shortened stickblade to improve his. And Mark Messier uses it more than any player in the NHL. Curved sticks have almost eliminated the backhand shot from the game, so goalies don't expect it. The backhand motion tells goalies to expect the puck to go high. Shooters who can keep their backhand shots down can score a lot of goals.

How to do it

The backhand shot is done exactly the same as the wrist shot, but from the other side of your body. Use the same sweeping motion with your stick, the same wrist snap, the same weight transfer from skate to skate and the same follow-through.

Jordan sneaks a peek at his target from the corner of his eye.

Power comes from upper body uncoiling and weight shift.

Keep it smooth. Keep the shot low by following through low.

The backhand shot

Body position: Concentrate on dropping your front shoulder to get the stickblade flat on the ice.

Follow-through: A low follow-through keeps your backhand low.

Backhand checklist

- Just do it. Half the battle is trying the backhand shot.
- Get your body into it. Start with your front (lower) shoulder down. Keep your upper hand in close.
- Don't flip the puck. Drive it. Follow through low.

How to do it

You should wait to work on your slap shot. It is hard on you, hard on your stick and hard to control, and the windup takes time. But who wants to wait? What a feeling you get! What power! What a noise! If you're going to practise it, you might as well do it right.

Body position: The puck is opposite your front foot. Look at the puck, not the target. Keep your head down all the way.

Hands: Grip your stick firmly with your top hand. Slide your lower hand down the shaft as you reach back, then lock that hand.

The shot: Your weight will shift naturally to your front foot as you swing. Feel the entire force of your arms and shoulders behind the shot as your weight moves forward. Your stickblade should hit the ice just behind the puck, which you want to hit near the heel. Snap your wrists at the moment of impact.

The slap shot

Eyes on the puck. Breathe in. Keep your backswing low to get the shot off faster.

Get your body into it. Contact the ice a couple of inches behind the puck.

Continue the body twist. All weight on your front skate. Aim at the target.

Follow-through: Follow through as far as you want. Keep all your weight on your front foot as you swing your stickblade at the target. How high a slap shot goes depends on where in your swing you hit the puck—the further forward you hit it, the higher it will go.

Slap shot checklist

- Where is the puck? Look.
- Keep your head down until you follow through.
- Hit the ice a few inches/centimetres behind the puck.

"For me, follow-through is the thing. It's like throwing a ball. You're aiming at the target. If you want to hit the far corner—aim for the far corner. It's the key to the success of my slap shot."

CAM NEELY

Brett Hull's secret is no secret at all: get the shot off fast and get it on the net. Quickness beats power. Accuracy beats the goalie. Always hit the net.

The snap shot is a scorer's secret weapon, the quickest shot you can get away. And you can shoot from close to your feet, so there is almost no windup, and no warning. It is a combination wrist and slap shot.

The snap shot takes more practise than other shots. Work on shooting off all the points along a tight quarter-circle, running from your forehand side next to your front foot to right in front of your feet, with your front foot pointed out. Breathe out hard on the power stroke to add explosiveness.

A crisp snap shot gives you the element of surprise—by enabling you to shoot from a crowd. It is tough to master, but very rewarding.

How to do it

Body position: The puck can be anywhere on your forehand side, even in front of you. You can be moving sideways across the goalmouth. It's also a great one-timer shot off a pass.

> ***T I P***
> Bend your knees on the follow-through to keep your balance.

Michelle's weight is on her inside leg all the way.

The shot is released in front of the feet, before the goalie is ready.

Her body twists to add power. This is a classic snap shot.

The snap shot

Hands: Bring your stickblade back on the ice. Keep your wrists cocked on the power stroke, and your follow-through short. Contact point: middle of the blade. Stroke: short, but explosive.
Follow-through: Keep your balance; many players fall backward after the forward weight transfer. The rear foot often leaves the ice during the follow-through, so be aware of checkers nearby.

Winning faceoffs usually means winning the game. If there are 50–60 faceoffs in a game, both teams have that many opportunities to take the puck and score.

Winning most of the faceoffs makes it possible to do other good things. In your own zone, it allows your team to make the safe play by freezing the puck or icing it. Offensively, forwards can go full speed and risk offsides knowing they will win the faceoff. Winning faceoffs in your opponents' zone can lead to quick goals.

Everyone should learn how to take faceoffs. You never know when the call might come. Even if you haven't done it much, you can make sure you don't lose. By attacking your opponent's stick, or by blocking the puck with your skate, anyone can avoid losing most faceoffs. In your own zone, remember to stay with the opposing centre until your team has the puck.

The trick to faceoffs is to study the officials and the opposing centres. How does the linesman drop the puck? Flat? Does it bounce? What is your opponent trying to do? What do you want to do?

Don't commit to the faceoff until you are ready. Take a deep breath, check your teammates, place your stick on the edge of the dot and look at the official's hand . . .

FACEOFFS

"Go into every faceoff positive: I'm going to win this draw. Know what you're going to do well in advance. Make *sure* you're balanced on your skates. And concentrate on the official's hand."

ADAM OATES

What to do

Every faceoff is different. What you do depends on the situation and where the faceoff is. Near the opposition's goal, be more aggressive. In your own zone, make sure you don't lose the draw.

1. Place your stick lightly on the ice at the edge of the dot with your lower hand down 3 or 4 inches/8–10 cm from your normal grip. Balance on both skates, toes straight ahead. As you put your stick down, look first at your opponent's feet, then at the official.

2. Watch the opposing centres and officials. Does the official pull his skate away just before he drops the puck? Is the other centre cheating with his or her feet? Those feet tell you a lot. For example, if your opponent has a forehand shot toward your net and the outside foot forward, it could be a direct shot off the faceoff. You block the stick.

Winning faceoffs

Jordan, the home-team centre, is checking his opponent's feet. No clues there this time.

Once he commits to the faceoff, he focuses totally on the referee's hand.

3. If your opponent is faster and you have to attack the stick, concentrate on a point about 4 inches/10 cm up the shaft. Lift it and either get your stick to the puck first or play it with your skates. If you lose, stay with the opposing centre. Be ready to lift your rival's stick when the puck comes to him or her.

4. You don't always have to use your stick to control the puck. You can attack your opponent's stick, get good body position, and kick the puck back to your defenseman. Or just tie up your opponent until help arrives.

Take command

Be a coach in the faceoff circle. In your own zone, let the goaltender know if you intend to draw the puck toward your net. Take a look at your goalie's equipment. Are his or her bottom straps loose?

Choking up on your stick makes you faster on the draw.

Be positive. Know what you are going to do. In your defensive zone it is more important not to lose the faceoff than to win it cleanly. To avoid losing, lift your opponent's stick and step into him or her. Play the puck with your skates. Stay with your opponent until your team gets the puck.

If you win, skate to the outside around your opposing centre, curl toward the middle with your stick on the ice and look for the breakout pass.

Jordan wins with a simple forehand move, swinging his left skate around to protect the puck.

But Jesse adjusts. He lifts Jordan's stick, leaving the puck up for grabs.

The key points

Faceoff checklist

- Once in the circle, check your teammates before you commit. Move them if necessary. You are in charge.
- Know what you are going to do.
- Hold your stick normally. A reversed lower hand signals your intentions.
- Is your opponent cheating? Check if his or her stick is down, or if one skate is forward. If so, back off.
- Watch the official's hand.

Scoring goals is fun. Some players can score goals all by themselves. But to win games, your team must keep your opponents from scoring.

You need many different skills to play defensive hockey. Your own defensive skills become part of the team's defense, because while one player can score by himself, no one player can prevent an opposing team from scoring. All six players on the team without the puck are defenders.

The first thing to know about playing defense is that all five skaters must work together. Learning defensive skills will make you a more complete hockey player, and make your team a better team. Although not every player can be a goal scorer, every player can learn how to defend.

D E F

His work ethic has made Scott Stevens a complete player. Controlling his temper keeps him on the ice longer. Know your weaknesses. Get rid of them.

There are three things your team has to do when the other team has the puck, and three sets of skills you use to get the puck back. Three things the team must do, three things you can do.

As a team, you have to:

1. Protect the middle lane. The shortest route to your team's goal is a straight line down the centre of the ice. If you can keep your opponents wide, along the boards, they are less likely to score.

2. Limit the amount of time and space available to your opponent. The faster you can get to the puck carrier, the less time and space that player has to make a play. Know who your check is, and stay no more than two stick lengths away, even when your check does not have the puck.

Line up your outside shoulder with the shooter's inside shoulder. Let the goalie see.

Watch the puck, and keep track of your check with your stick. Stay within one or two stick lengths.

Team defense

3. Prevent your opponents from scoring. Your opponents are most likely to score from within your team's defensive zone. Stay within two stick lengths of your check. Keep between your check and the net in the defensive zone, and between your check and the puck in other areas of the ice.

4. Good defense pays off when your team gets the puck. The change from offense to defense happens quickly in hockey. The switch from checker to pass receiver can happen in an instant. Learn to read the change and react fast.

You need three individual skills to take the puck from an opposing player. The one you use depends on the situation. Which zone are you in? Is the puck carrier your check? Are you alone or is there help nearby? Is the puck carrier coming to you, or do you have to go to the puck? The three individual skills you need are:

Body contact: The player with the puck can be stopped through body contact—not body checking, but other forms of contact, such as blocking the path of the puck carrier.

Stick-checks: Or you can take the puck away by stick-checks. There are many kinds of stick-checks, from lifting an opponent's stick with yours to sweeping the puck away with your stick.

Positioning and angling: Or you can approach a puck-carrying opponent in a way that makes the puck carrier do what you want. In other words, you decide where you want your opponent to go with the puck, and you overplay the side you don't want him or her to go to.

This is called positioning and angling. You read whether your opponent has control of the puck, and you react to that by making that player do what you want him or her to do.

INDIVIDUAL SKILLS

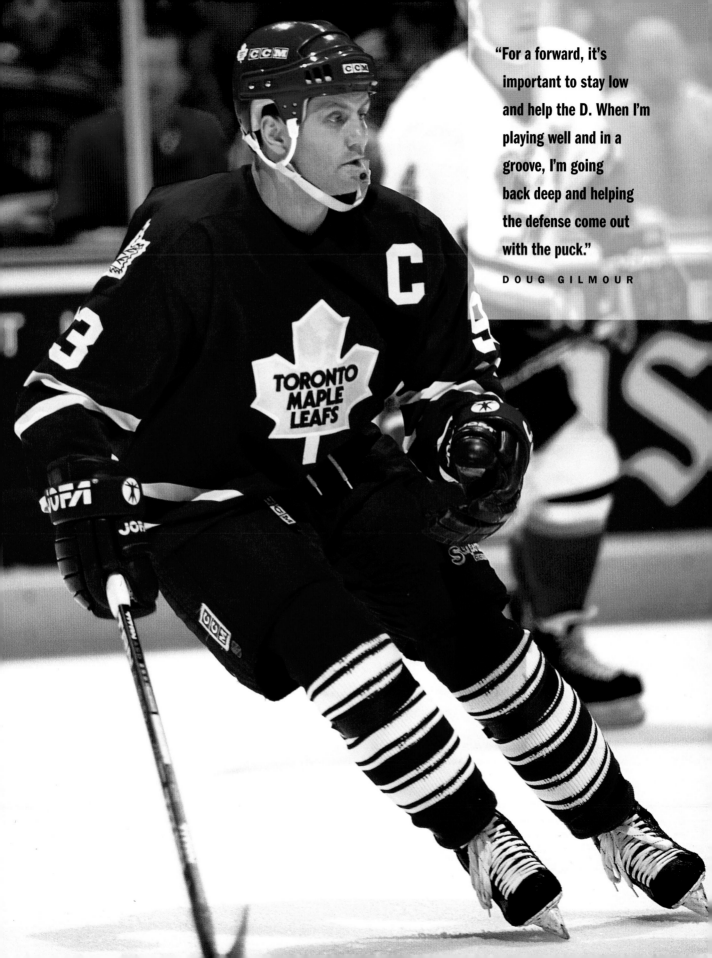

"For a forward, it's important to stay low and help the D. When I'm playing well and in a groove, I'm going back deep and helping the defense come out with the puck."

DOUG GILMOUR

How to do it

Sooner or later, especially if you are in your own zone and you are positioned between your check and your goal, the opposing puck carrier has to bring the puck to you. To get the puck away from your opponent, body contact and stick-checks can be used close up.

But what happens when the other team has control of the puck and they are not coming anywhere near you? (This is usually the case when the puck is in their zone.) If you are the defensive player closest to the puck, positioning and angling helps you attack the puck carrier.

Positioning

Positioning refers to where you should be on the ice. In your zone, for example, you are between the puck carrier and your goal.

Positioning & angling

The forechecker reads the defenseman's number. That means attack the puck. Go after it.

The defenseman has control of the puck. Contain. Play the pass.

> **T I P**
> Always have a plan when you go to the puck. Never approach the puck carrier head-on. Come at the puck from an angle.

Angling

Angling is how you approach the puck carrier to get him or her to do what you want. For example: by angling toward an opposition defenseman from the middle on the forecheck, you invite the defenseman to pass up the boards. The following forechecker, reading your angle, can anticipate that pass up the boards and go for the puck.

This is a time to read and react. You must read how well your opponent is controlling the puck, and react. Your teammates must read what you are doing, and react to take advantage.

If you see your opponent's sweater crest, he or she probably has good control of the puck. Seeing this, you contain the puck carrier. Take away their best option—usually the pass into the middle. Angle toward the puck carrier from the middle of the ice.

On the forecheck, if the puck carrier does not pass, force him or her back behind the net by attacking from the outside. That gives your teammates time to pick up their checks, making an effective pass more difficult.

If you see your opponent's number, he or she does not yet have control. Pressure the puck carrier. Go to the puck. This is your chance to get possession.

The sweater-crest-or-number rule always applies on the forecheck in the offensive zone, and also on many defensive zone one-on-ones (for example, when approaching an opposing forward

The deep forechecker takes away the middle lane. The defenseman passes up the boards.

The second forechecker reads the pass and reacts by going to the boards.

Positioning & angling

with the puck in a corner of your zone). Positioning and angling enables you to dictate what the puck carrier can do, so your team can take advantage.

This is where teamwork comes in. The second player on the forecheck must read what his or her teammate is inviting the puck carrier to do, and react by going where the puck will go. If the first forechecker can take the puck or that second player can intercept the pass, the two forecheckers will have a good chance to score.

You are now close to the puck carrier on the forecheck, or the puck carrier is coming at you in your own zone. This is the moment to take the puck.

Poke-check

This is the best move to use when the puck carrier is approaching you head-on. Hold your stick with your top hand only, and thrust directly at the puck, with your stickblade flat on the ice. Don't lose your balance.

Sweep-check

This check works best from in front or slightly to one side against a good stickhandler. Instead of poking directly at the puck, sweep your stick low to the ice so it hits the puck carrier's stick.

Stick-checks

Poke-check. Go right at the puck, top hand only on the stick.

Sweep-check. Covers more ice, and forces the puck carrier to get rid of the puck.

T I P

Be very careful not to lift your opponent's stick above waist level. This is how many stick-related injuries occur.

Stick lift

Use a stick lift when approaching an opposing puck carrier from behind or at an angle. Move your lower hand down your stick for leverage. Lift your opponent's stick from low on the shaft, skate through the puck, and pick it up with your back skateblade.

Stick press

The opposite of lifting your opponent's stick. Just use your stick to press your opponent's stick down. Aim for the blade-to-handle joint.

Body checking is not allowed at your age level. But body contact will take place when 10 people, all of them after one puck, are skating in a confined area. The ability to make legal contact is an important skill in hockey. It is also a good way to prepare yourself for full-contact hockey in a few years' time.

Blocking the way

It is legal for a defender to block the way of the puck carrier— as long as the defender is in the lane first. You can not step into the puck carrier's path.

In your own zone, getting between your check and the net is your first task. If your check gets the puck and you are in position, you will be blocking the way. This is hard to do. But being in the puck carrier's way makes you a good defensive player.

T I P

It is important to learn how to control offensive players without hitting them, no matter what level of hockey you are playing. Good defensive skills are often the key to moving up to the next level.

The checker can simply skate the puck carrier off the puck and take control.

Leaning into the puck carrier along the boards is legal . . .

. . . and so is simply stepping between the puck carrier and the puck.

Body contact

Leaning into the puck carrier

If you and the puck carrier are going in the same direction, you can lean into him or her. You may even be able to deflect the puck carrier from his or her path. Keep your feet moving to stay with the puck carrier. To prevent a penalty, do not hook or hold your opponent.

At your playing level, you can not finish a check by running the puck carrier into the boards. In fact, you can't check anyone but the puck carrier.

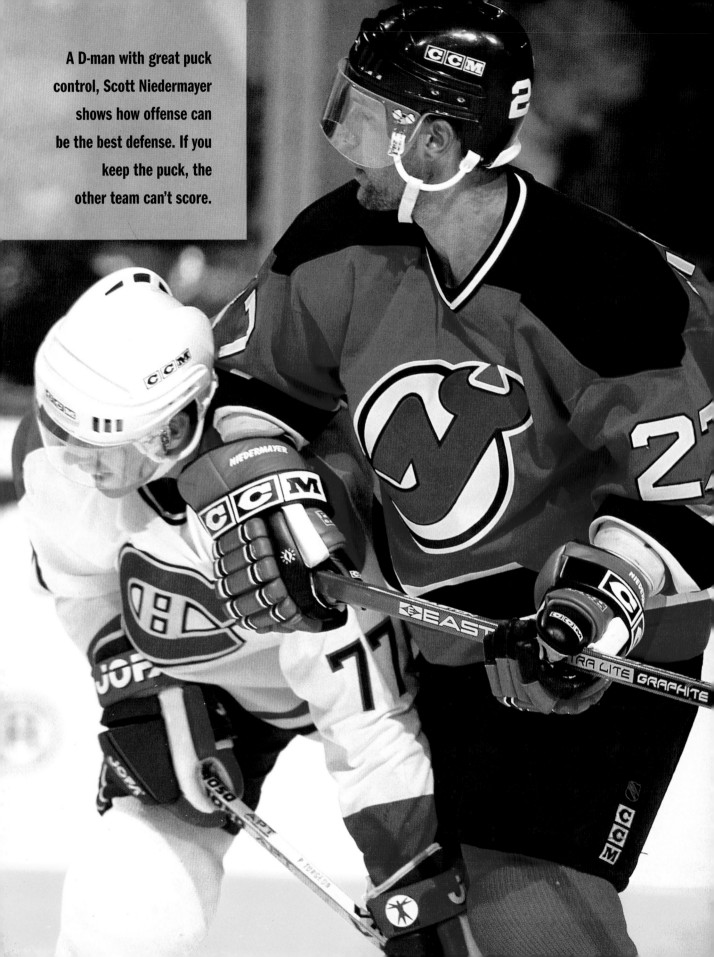

A D-man with great puck control, Scott Niedermayer shows how offense can be the best defense. If you keep the puck, the other team can't score.

Any stick-to-stick action creates danger. *You* are to blame for any damage your stick causes when you are doing anything other than handling the puck. Be careful with your stick. It is most useful when the blade is on the ice.

- Never carry your stick high. The puck moves on the ice; you can't play it with your stick in the air. But you can hurt someone badly when you carry your stick high.

- Never use the butt end of your stick on an opponent.

- Never push an opponent from behind along the boards. Observe a 4-foot/1.2-m safety zone along the boards.

- Never bump an opponent within the 4-foot/1.2-m safety zone. Play the *puck* along the boards, not the player.

A high stick hurts your opponent, your team, or both. Don't take the risk.

Butt-ending is a cheap shot that can cost you big time in penalties.

Hitting from behind can leave your opponent paralyzed for life.

The nevers of defensive play

It takes a special kind of individual to play goal. You have to be the kind of person who takes charge.

In the end, you want to be a goaltender so the job will get done right. You are the only player who can't take the night off. You want to be where the action is and you are willing to learn from your mistakes. You must also be in control of your emotions.

Taking responsibility means never, ever, blaming others for the goals you give up. Always support the defense—especially when they are having a bad game. Your job is to correct your teammates' mistakes by making the save.

That's what makes the goaltender the most important player on the team. But you know that. That's why you're a goalie.

GOAL

ED BELFOUR

ENDING

Styles in goaltending come and go. Goalies usually develop their own unique style by finding out what works best for them, and by watching other netminders. Every style has strengths and weaknesses. Most goalies, however, play a combination of the following three styles:

Stand-up

The classic high-percentage style, stand-up goaltending requires good footwork to move sideways. Even a stand-up goalie like Kirk McLean goes to his knees to make half of his saves. Other stand-up goalies: Bill Ranford, Jeff Hackett.

Strengths: Less of a five-hole; good lateral and in-and-out movement; best for controlling rebounds; enables a goalie to move the puck quickly.

Weaknesses: Lower corners uncovered; screen shots can be a problem. Angles must be perfect.

Butterfly

This style gets its name from the way some goalies go to their knees with leg pads spread outward to cover most of the goalmouth ice surface. Tom Barrasso, Patrick Roy and Andy Moog are butterfly goalies who have won Stanley Cups.

Strengths: A good style against screen shots or low deflections. Good for freezing the puck—you are already down.

Weaknesses: Timing is important. When you go to your knees, you can't move with the play; pad saves create rebounds in front; shooters will go high on you.

Inverted-V

These goalies stand with their feet apart and knees together, showing the five-hole open. But just try to score there on Grant Fuhr, Ed Belfour or Felix Potvin! The inverted-V combines aspects of the other two styles; you are on your feet more of the time, but closer to being in the butterfly.

Strengths: A gambling, great-save style. A natural style for reflex goalies. Gets your bulk in the way of more shots—the puck hits inverted-V goalies a lot. Ideal for covering the ice on scrambles by putting the wide part of your stick on the ice.

Weaknesses: This style puts you deep in the crease, which often means bad-angle goals. Having your knees together locks your skates on the inside edges, making sideways movement difficult.

Styles

"The most important thing about the stand-up style is having good balance. The advantage of the stand-up style is on the second shot. You're always in a position to make that second save."

BILL RANFORD

By being in line with the shooter, a goalie covers as much of the net as possible. Being on the line a shot must travel to enter the net is called "playing the angle."

Position is everything with a goalie. The best goalies seem to move very little; the puck seems attracted to them. Goalies who often get hit by the puck are playing their angles right.

There are two aspects to playing angles: side-to-side movements and gliding in and out of the net.

All players learn to move forward, backward and sideways. But the goalie must do so without changing his or her stance. As a goalie, you must move ahead without pumping your arms and shoulders, move back without swinging your hips and move sideways without opening the five-hole too wide. You must learn to move in any direction without lifting your stickblade off the ice.

The key is staying in your stance. Nothing about goaltending is easy, but moving around while keeping square to the shooter and in your stance is your biggest step toward becoming a reliable goaltender. Know how your stickside arm feels when your stickblade is flat on the ice and be aware of that feeling. Most goals are scored with the goalies out of their stances for some reason.

ANGLES & MOVEMENT

"The butterfly is the position where you cover the most surface of the ice. I know 60 per cent of the goals are scored on the ice. If I can't cover the ice I'm in trouble."

PATRICK ROY

If the shooter is in the slot—between the circles and directly in front of the net—the goalie should be midway between the posts. As the shooter moves to one side or the other, the goalie follows. Always be on the line the puck has to travel to enter the centre of the net.

How to do it

How you move from side-to-side depends on how far away the puck is.

With the puck well out, shuffle by taking a sideways step with the foot on the side you want to move toward, then bring the other foot along to close the pads. Repeat until you are in position. Keep square to the shooter.

With the puck in close, do a T-push for a quicker, smoother movement. Turn the foot on the side you want to move toward sideways, then push in that direction with the other skate.

Side-to-side

Brandon moves to his right without losing his stance.

Shuffle across the goalmouth in short sideways steps, keeping track of the play.

To get across faster, the T-push is the ticket. Keep your stick on the ice.

To stop, lean back. The back foot will act as a brake. Learn to move quickly from goalpost to goalpost in one easy T-push glide.

Either way, shuffle or T-push, stay square to the shooter until the shot is on its way. Turn sideways only to make the save. Present as much of your equipment to the shooter as possible. Stay in your stance as long as you can.

When the puck is far away from the net, move out. As the puck moves to one side, back up toward the net and to that side. Or, if a lone shooter comes in on the wing, move out to challenge the shooter. If no shot comes, move back toward the net as the shooter passes the circle hash marks, in case the shooter tries to go around you.

How to do it

A goalie glides in and out with small movements of the ankles and feet. That is why goaltenders have to be good skaters. They must move around the ice as quickly as other players, but without using their bodies for leverage. All the power is generated from the knees down.

Ian Young, a respected goaltending coach, calls the in-and-out movement "telescoping." As you move toward the shooter, you get bigger and block more of the net.

> **T I P**
> *Come out* to play the shot, then *back in* to play the deke.

Kendall's solid stance and correct angle on the puck allows her to cover a lot of the net from inside the crease . . .

. . . but she covers almost all of it by coming out on a line with the puck. Go for the top corner? She dares you.

In & out

As with every rule in goaltending, there is an exception. If an opposition player appears to either side of you, you must cheat back to the net and a bit toward that side. Sometimes goalies have to do two things at once. You still focus on the shooter, as always. Don't be distracted. Stay on the line of the shot. Stopping the shot is still your main job. But be ready to react to the pass.

Up or down?

Today a goalie has to be able to play both ways. Always stay up and keep your stance until the shooter commits. Keep your body and padding upright so shots can hit you. Remember, you can only move when you are on your feet. That way, you are ready for the first shot, the second shot, and any other shots coming your way.

But when things get hot near the net, be like Felix Potvin and get as much of your equipment as possible along the ice. You can see the puck better from down low, too. The puck bounces around more on low shots. In close, it is harder for the shooter to hit the top corners.

If the question is "Up or down?" the answer is "Both." It depends on where the puck is.

Up & down

Many goalies bend too much at the waist. Bend at the knees and keep your upper body up, so the puck can hit it.

You see more of the puck through legs than through bodies. Get low on screen shots.

T I P
The key to goaltending success in all situations: always let the puck play *you*.

Goaltending checklist

- Above all else, keep your eye on the puck. Find the puck. Don't make excuses for yourself on screened shots.
- Keep your stickblade on the ice. Know how your stick should feel when you're in your normal stance. Goalies most often lift their stickblades off the ice when crossing the net, when charging out or when expecting a high shot, such as a backhand.
- Be on your feet at the post. Bad-angle goals are scored because the goalie is down.

So far we've been talking about the simplest situation: goalie versus shooter. But what if the shooter passes to a teammate?

How to do it

Throwing yourself feet-first across the goalmouth is one way to make great saves against two or more opponents.

Push off the same way you would in a T-push, then flex the knee you push off with. Lead with the pad on the side you are moving toward. Concentrate on getting the push-off pad—the lower pad as you cross the goalmouth—flat on the ice fast. Don't fall on your bottom elbow. That keeps your upper body off the ice, and it's hard on your elbows.

Your stick is important. If stacking to your stick side, hold it above your top pad, adding to the goalmouth area you have

> **T I P**
>
> The key is to get as as much ice surface covered as soon as possible. Get that lower pad down flat. Then get your upper body down—fast.

Because a goalie has glove and stick sides, stacking the pads is a bit different each way.

Either way, Kendall is blocking the low shot and any possible pass across the goalmouth.

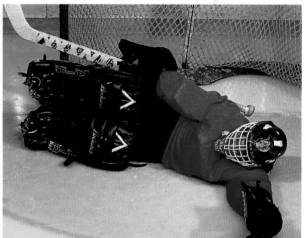

Stacking the pads

covered. Stacking to your glove side, get the wide part of your stick flat on the ice to cover the surface as your body falls.

Finish with your body flat across the goalmouth. Often a pass receiver at the open side will deflect the puck back toward the middle of the goalmouth, figuring your body will be the last part of you on the ice. Get everything down fast!

Resist the urge to kick out to show yourself you've made the save. That creates a rebound. Usually the puck will be under you. Just wait. Listen. You'll soon know if you made the save.

Goaltending is based on reactions. You react to the play because there isn't time to think in the net. Well-chosen drills simulate game situations. By doing drills over and over again, goalies develop the right reactions to a variety of situations.

Five-point drill

First, pick a player to be the "coach." The goalies then face the "coach." With a stick, the "coach" points left, right, forward or backward. Goalies move in the direction indicated until the direction changes. Be careful to maintain your stance throughout the drill.

A variation is to add Up and Down. The "coach" points a stickblade up or down and shouts "Hit the deck!" Work on getting back up fast.

Post-to-post

A passer has the puck behind the net. That player can pass from either side of the net into the slot, or put the puck on the net if you're not at the post fast enough. Try to block the pass with your stick.

Post-to-slot

A passer is behind the goal line, 10 feet/3 m to the side of the net. He can either shoot from there, to make sure you are hugging the post, or pass to the shooter in front.

If it's a pass, push off the post and centre yourself at the top of the crease before the shot comes. You can't stop a well-aimed shot to either corner while moving (your skateblades can't be turned sideways when you're moving forward).

Showdown

Most goalies love showdowns. Shooters come in on breakaways, and you try to stop them. See if you can stop them more often than they can score.

Movement drills

The goalie is like a catcher in baseball. You are the only player on your team with a full view of the ice. You should read plays as they develop, call them out to your teammates, and then react yourself.

Before the attackers enter your zone—especially if some of them are waiting at the blueline—think dump-in. If you see an opponent at the boards about to shoot straight ahead, start out on that side of your net to field the shoot-around. Be ready to handle a bad bounce with your skates. Always return by the same side you leave your net.

Most goals are scored within seconds of the opposing team entering your zone, so get into your stance when they cross centre. Know if your team is outnumbered at the blueline. Be well out, centred or slightly to the side, depending on where your opponents cross the blueline. Be ready for the long shot.

If your team is outnumbered at your blueline, call it out: "*two*-on-one," or *three*-on-one." That lets your teammates know you are in the game and committed to the puck carrier. They know they can play the pass.

Once the opposition is in your zone, let the puck play you. Let it pull you out of the net, or draw you from side to side. Let the puck be your friend. Welcome it when it comes to you.

GAME SITUATIONS

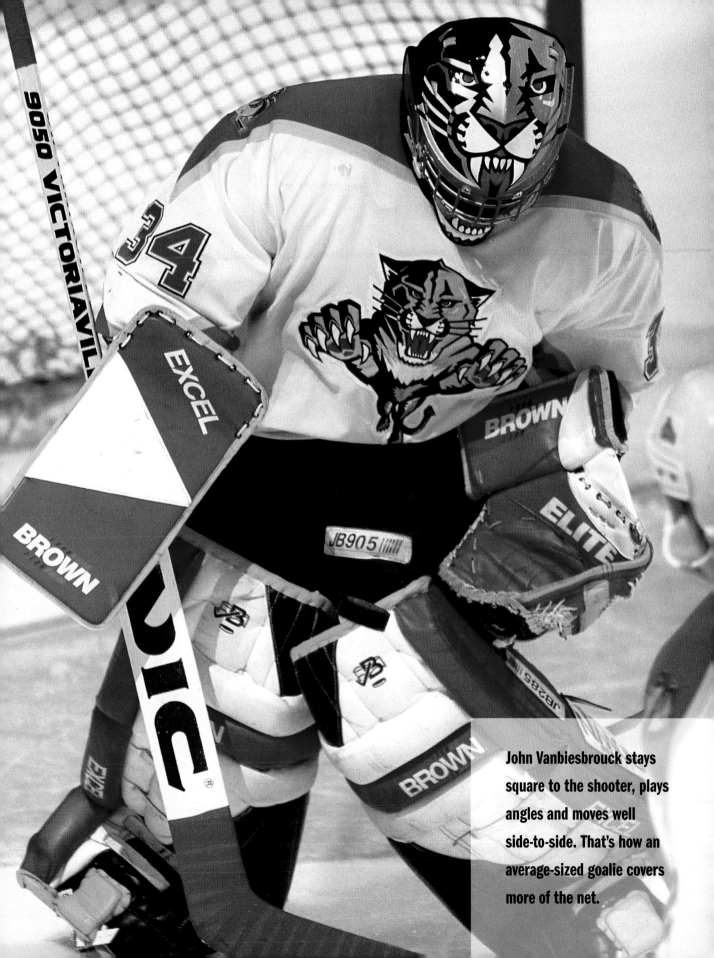

John Vanbiesbrouck stays square to the shooter, plays angles and moves well side-to-side. That's how an average-sized goalie covers more of the net.

Two-on-one

Call it out to the defenseman: *"Two*-on-one."

Two things can happen. The puck carrier can shoot or pass. You cover the shot. Your defenseman is watching for the pass. If the shooter shows signs of wanting to pass, fine. But you are committed to the shooter as long as that player has the puck and is moving toward the net. Don't anticipate, but be aware of the open player.

As soon as the puck carrier passes, react. What you do depends on how close the pass receiver is.

Far out: If the pass is far out of your reach, T-push across, staying on your feet.

In close: If the puck is in close, you may be able to deflect the pass. If not, stack your pads: slide feet-first to the far post.

On the rush

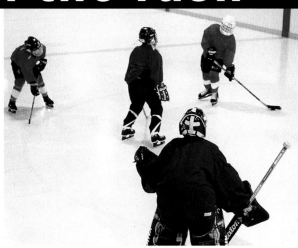

On a two-on-one rush, the goalie plays the shooter. Leave the pass to the defenseman . . .

. . . until the other attacker has the puck. Try to come across on your feet—if possible.

If the pass is close enough, try to kick out with your lower leg pad before that player can redirect the puck. Don't think about it. Stacking your pads is an instinctive, split-second reaction.

Three-on-one

Make sure it *is* a three-on-one. Is somebody getting back to cancel part of the advantage? If not, call it out. Play deep in your net. Play the shooter, but not as aggressively. Respond to a pass as you would on a two-on-one, but stay on your feet.

Breakaways

All the pressure is on the shooter. This is a read-and-react situation for the netminder. An early clue is where the shooter is carrying the puck. Is the puck to the side or in front? Side means shot. Front means deke.

First, think shot. Be well out beyond the crease and in line with the puck. Take away the shot. You want the shooter to deke. If there is an angle, the closer the shooter gets the more you play the forehand shot. Watch for a defenseman coming back who can take one side away from the puck carrier.

Once the shooter comes into the 10-foot/3-m zone stick-handling with the puck in front, it's a deke. Now you have the edge. Hold your ground. Don't go for the deke. Make the puck carrier commit to one side or the other.

T I P
The closer the puck carrier comes, the more likely it's a deke. Let the shooter make the first move.

Be well out of the net to take away the shot, but not too far to get back in . . .

The puck carrier is coasting in shooting position. Hold your ground . . .

The shooter decides to deke. Wait for him or her to commit, then react.

Breakaways

Once the puck carrier has committed to one side, don't overreact. Often your opponent will tuck the puck under you as soon as you open your legs. Keep your stickblade on the ice and between your legs. Depending on your style, play the move with your pad or skateblade. Keep your glove ready for the flip shot.

Remember, once your opponents are established in your zone—as in a power play—read the play. Try to stay on your feet. Let the puck play you. Making the breakaway save can turn a game around. Nothing feels better.

Point shots

How you play a point shot depends on what is going on around you. An unchecked opponent to your side forces you back into your net, to guard the back door. An unchecked opponent in front of you forces you to get as close as possible behind that player, to smother the deflection.

Take control. When your team can't get the puck out of your zone, you are the only one who can give them a breather. Sooner or later the puck will come to you. Cover up. Get the faceoff.

Faceoffs in your zone

Be ready for anything. How is your centre doing on draws? If the opposing centre has a forehand shot toward you, beware of a shot right off the drop.

In your zone

Be well out for a point shot. Take away as much net as possible . . .

. . . until another opponent appears. You still play the shot, but cheat back into your net. Don't let that open player get behind you for the easy tip-in.

Most often, the opposing centre will try to draw the puck back to a shooter near the slot. How the centre holds a stick tells you a lot.
- Reversed lower hand = draw back.
- Normal grip + forehand toward you = shot.

Check your equipment during the pause. Look for loose foot straps. Let the official know if you're not ready. Find the shooter before the puck drops to see which way he or she shoots. Make sure your centre checks with you before committing to the faceoff. Then focus—totally—on the drop of the puck.

Wraparounds

When your opponents have possession behind your net, keep your stance. Do not turn around. Look back over your shoulders.

To get to the opposite post, T-push across in one push off the near post, then turn the toe of your lead skate inward so the puck can't be banked in off your skateblade. Move your stick ahead of you and past the far post, but keep the blade open (not parallel to the goal line) on the way across. This is so that the puck carrier can't bank the puck off your stick into the net. Turn the stickblade slightly out from the goalmouth on the way across and then turn it square to the puck carrier once it is outside the post.

Reach ahead with your stick as you move across. You can prevent passouts just by having your stick outside the post before you get there.

Kendall is waiting, skateblade against the post, as Will comes around from behind. No chance . . .

. . . so he goes the other way. Kendall is already there, ready to poke-check the puck off his stick.

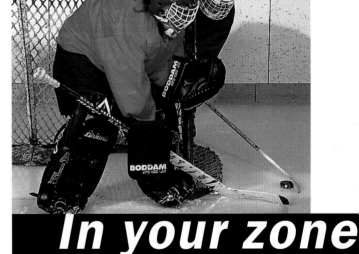

In your zone

In-your-zone checklist

- If you lose sight of the puck, get low. You can see through legs better than through bodies.
- When your team is losing faceoffs in your end, cheat toward the shooter—unless the opposing centre has a forehand shot on you.
- Are your teammates running around after the puck? Be cool. They need you more than ever now.
- Thank your defense for big plays. Nobody else will notice.

Warmups

The warmup is a dangerous time for any goalie. No goalie steps on the ice ready to play. Before every game or practice, you have to get used to being hit with the puck. That means easy shots to begin with. Make sure your teammates keep all shots low. There is no excuse for shooting high or deking a cold goalie.

Some goalies start games angry at their teammates for trying to score in warmups, or for shooting high or missing the net. It is normal to feel upset when that happens. But don't argue with your teammates during a bad warmup, and try to put it behind you when the game begins. Let the coach know how you feel, though. A well-organized warmup keeps everybody focused, busy and productive.

Focus points

TIP
When you shout warnings or commands to your teammates, sound confident, and be precise. Never sound panicky.

Communication on the ice

Like the catcher in baseball, the goalie is the only one on the playing surface with a complete view of the game. You can help your defense by warning them of danger or pointing out opportunities. But remember: You are shouting through a mask. Your warning has to be simple and clear.

- The most helpful information you can give a teammate is whether he or she is under pressure. Yell "Man on you!" when there is a checker right behind your teammate. If your teammate has lots of time, yell "You got time!" or "No pressure."

- Defenders are not always aware when they are screening you. Yell "Screen! Screen! Screen!" Make it urgent.

- On an opposition rush where your defense is outnumbered, call out the situation, like "*two*-on-one" or "*three*-on-one." If a backchecker gets back to cancel the disadvantage, let the defense know they can take the puck carrier: "Take him! / Take her!"

- Signal the end of a penalty by banging your stickblade flat on the ice so the penalized player can't sneak in behind your power-play point shooter.

How does Dominik Hasek do it? How does he stop more shots than other goalies? He sees the puck well. He has quick feet. He directs rebounds to the side.

"I would say I butterfly a lot. I like to play the angle and challenge the shooters. I don't *over*challenge, but I do play angles. I play that way so I can try and get close to the ice, where most of the shots go."

FELIX POTVIN

Think about it

- Prepare for the game before you get to the dressing room. Be there before anyone else. Do your stretching at home, and leave yourself lots of time at the arena to get your equipment just right. Be ready five or 10 minutes before the warmup.

- Maintain your concentration on the ice. There are many ways to do this. Kirk McLean tries to get into a rhythm by listening to rock music and getting into the beat. Some goalies divide the game into five-minute segments. Breathe in positive fresh air during breaks in the play, and breathe out the negative stuff.

- Goals scored on you early in the game put your team in a hole. When the others aren't ready to play, you have to be. If you can keep your team in the game early, chances are they will respond. But if the hole is too deep, they can't climb out.

- Consistency is more important than making the big save. The trick is to keep things simple. Let the puck play you, even in the offensive end. Move with it. Think basics: seal off the posts, be aware of your stick on the ice, watch your angles. Bad goals result from forgetting the basics.

- Never lie on the ice after the score to show you had no chance. Don't bang your stick on the ice or the goalpost in anger. Control yourself. Don't ever let your opponents know they are getting to you.

The mind game

- Take responsibility for the goals scored on you. But don't blame yourself. There is a difference. Know what you should have done to prevent them, but don't dwell on mistakes. Give yourself a break. Stay positive. There will be plenty of chances to redeem yourself. Your confidence has to withstand bad goals.

- Every goalie has bad games. The best ones don't make bad games worse.

- Always be in the game enough to learn. When the play is in the other end, study your opposing goaltender. Even if you think you are better, find something in his or her game to learn from.

Hockey's main disadvantage, compared with other sports, is the high cost of equipment. It usually costs up to $500 to equip a player at the skating positions, and twice that for a goalie. One reason equipment costs so much is that it has improved a great deal—in both protection and durability. But because hockey equipment lasts well, it makes sense to buy most of it secondhand.

The two places where it makes no sense to save money is at a player's head and feet. Head protection that does not fit is worse than none at all, because a bad fit alone can cause injuries. Skates that don't fit or that have lost their ability to protect can do serious harm to growing feet.

Equipment must do two things: fit and protect.

E Q U I

P M E N T

No piece of equipment can make you quit hockey faster than skates that don't fit. Good quality secondhand skates can save money, but it takes an experienced eye to find the good ones.

How to buy skates

1. Check the heel counter. Does it grip the heel tightly? Does it feel strong when you squeeze from outside?

2. Buy skates that fit. Don't buy skates that are too big, thinking you'll grow into them. Built-in support won't help you if two pairs of thick socks come between your feet and your skates. (If you have narrow feet, have a shoemaker add ankle support.) Wear a single pair of socks (many professionals play barefoot under their skates for a better feel). Always tap the heel of the foot into place by striking the back of the skateblade on a suitable surface.

Skates & sticks

There's no feeling like being ready a little early, in equipment that fits.

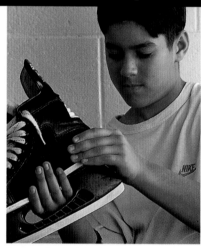

Jordan checks his skates for support in the all-important heel counter area.

He makes sure his heel is fully secured in its cup before he laces his skates ...

T I P
Avoid buying skates in the morning, when your feet are smaller.

3. Now lace—not too tight!—and stand. There should be no more than a quarter-inch/6-mm space at your toes; you should be able to move them sideways and up and down. If your big toe is touching the front of the boot, try a half-size or one size larger.

4. The blades. You want through-hardened steel, not case-hardened. Ask. Avoid too much rocker to your skateblade. If skates fit right, they don't have to be laced too tightly. Never wrap the laces around the ankle. Only the top three eyelets need to be tight. If your feet get cold when you play, your laces are too tight.

Lacing your skates

Lace your skates in the same crisscross style you use for your shoes. This allows the laces to move with your feet. Don't skip the top eyelets. You need the support.

Skate guards are cheap and they are a must. They protect both your skateblades and the rest of your equipment. Dry your blades with an oily cloth after every use. (Keep the cloth in a zip-lock bag.)

Your stick

No piece of equipment is as personal as your stick, and it doesn't have to be expensive. A little care and attention makes a big difference in how your stick works for you.

Length: If you are standing in your skates with your stick held up in front of you, the handle should extend only to your shoulder and

T I P

Most stickblades are so rounded that the lie number means little. Take the stick and get in your skating crouch to see if it feels right for you.

...tight but not too tight, laced in Xs so the boot can flex as he skates.

Jordan's stick may be a little long compared with some...

...but it feels right for him with its shallow lie and straight blade.

Skates & sticks

no higher. It can be shorter. In general, your stick should be as short as you can comfortably use.

Stick check: Look carefully at a stick you've been using. Is the wear on the tape even along the underside of the blade?

- If the wear is concentrated at the heel, switch to a shorter stick or a lower lie.
- If the wear is at the toe, you may need a longer stick, or one with a higher lie. A good first step is to try the higher lie and compensate by shortening the shaft.

Helmets & masks

Helmets and masks are tested by the hockey and product standards associations in your country. Make sure the ones you buy are approved. A helmet/wire mask combination is preferred because clear plastic visors are difficult to care for and scratch easily. Most hockey helmets can be adjusted for fit. They have moving parts that should be checked regularly, to make sure the screws and fasteners are secure.

Renovating a secondhand helmet

To remove minor stains and blemishes, wash with dishwashing detergent and polish with car wax. (For tougher nicks and scrapes, use Brasso metal polish, then wax.) Make sure all soft padding in the helmet is intact, or remove it before washing.

Other equipment

Michelle, a goalie and centre, looks for the approval stickers on both helmets.

If used hockey pants can stand on their own, there's life left in them.

Glove wrist guards and elbow pads should meet or overlap.

Pads & pants

Make sure the hard caps on shoulder and elbow pads are intact, and that fasteners, such as Velcro, have not lost their grip.

A common mistake is to buy pants that are too small, leaving an unprotected gap above the shinguard kneecap. Pants can be bought a bit large, to allow for growth. Make sure the protective padding and caps are in good shape. Hockey pants should have enough life left in them to stand on their own.

When choosing gloves, for basic protection the wrist guard should at least meet the bottom edge of your elbow pads.

Teemu Selanne scores
with his hands and feet.
He trades speed for goals.
He is constantly in motion.
His feet get him there.
His hands finish the job.

Goaltending equipment is expensive, and it has to fit perfectly. But many goaltenders take up their lonely occupation because they like the gear, so they are more likely to take care of the expensive tools of their trade.

Helmets & masks

A helmet/wire mask combination costs less and is easier to fit than the formfitted fibreglass model with fixed wire facemask. But the formfitted type, while much more expensive, protects the ears and throat better.

If you use a helmet/mask, make sure you have protection for your throat in the form of a padded collar-type strip, or hang a clear plastic shield from your mask, as Patrick Roy does. Make sure your wire mask extends back at the sides, over your ears.

Goaltending equipment

Michelle's goal mask and throat protector overlap, leaving no openings.

Used blockers are fine if the glove palm is fully intact.

Look for stiffness along the thumb and wrist guard of a used catching mitt.

Gloves

Secondhand gloves are fine, as long as the padding is still intact and lively. There should be some stiffness in the thumb, outside edge and cuff of the trapper, or catching glove, as well as padding for the back of the hand. A used stick-glove, or blocker, is built so rigidly that it usually needs only to be repalmed so that no fingers pop out. As a goalie, you'll want gloves as big as you can get them. But gloves that are too big are wasted if your hands are too small to control them.

Leg pads

Leg pads are the most important fitting problem for goalies, after helmets and skates. A general rule is that stand-up goalies use shorter pads and butterfly goalies longer ones. (Butterfly goalies, with their knees bent, expose a gap between their pants and pads.)

Your knee should line up with the middle one of the three horizontal rolls on the front of the leg pad. Anywhere above that, and the knee is vulnerable. Below, and the pads are too long for you to skate freely. Andy Moog's goaltending instruction video suggests that pads be no more than 6-8 inches/15-20 cm above the knee when a player is in street shoes.

Most youth hockey associations provide pads for goalies, but those pads have often seen better days. Secondhand pads,

Kendall's goal pads fit perfectly. Her knee meets the middle roll.

The first goal pad strap goes under the skate boot for good foot coverage.

Most goalies wear additional pads under their stockings to cover the knees.

Goaltending equipment

especially in smaller sizes, are widely available. Most goalies wear hard-capped pads on their knees under their leg pads to give protection when their knees are bent. Those pads should fit perfectly, and be in good condition; they can partly compensate for leg pads that are a little small. If a pucks hits your unprotected knee it could cripple you for life.

As a goalie, it is important that your leg pads cover the inside of your calves; the bottom straps should pass under the heels of your skates to protect your feet.

Road warriors

You've heard oldtimers talk about learning to play hockey by skating all day on frozen ponds. But there aren't many ponds in the city. Even when there are, they don't freeze if you live in southern California, Florida or Texas. Yet you can still play hockey all day if you want. Outdoors. And it costs no more than that old pond did.

Today you can play hockey on streets, lanes, basketball and tennis courts, empty parking lots and asphalt schoolyards— on any fairly smooth, hard surface. Cities have plenty of those. The edges are rougher than an ice rink's: brick and chain link instead of boards and glass. But roller hockey skates feel a lot like ice skates once you get used to the wider turns. Just lean more. And always remember to oil your bearings.

Will goes wheelin' with industrial-grade bearings for a smooth roll.

Roller hockey pads are made of ballistic nylon to provide a road-proof shell.

The well-dressed road warrior wears asphalt-resistant gear—black as tar.

In-line skating

The big difference between ice hockey and roller hockey? When you crash on ice, you're in for a ride. Tumble on tar, and road rash is the best you can hope for. So you want a road-proof shell on your elbows and knees, something made of kryptonite. Luckily, in-line hockey gear is made of aircraft materials that didn't exist 10 years ago. And most of it is lighter than regular hockey equipment.

The best part about roller hockey is, no adults allowed. Nobody telling you what to do. It's wide-open fun-in-the-sun hockey. Shoot the lights out. Score 'til you snore. Be there.

To keep in shape, eat well and play all the sports you can. Other sports teach skills, such as hand-eye co-ordination and agility, that are useful in hockey.

Running is the best all-round exercise you can get. But try to avoid running on roads and sidewalks—paved surfaces are hard on the ankles and knees. Swimming is another great way to build stamina.

It's less important which way you get fit, though, than how you do it. Paul Carson, who has played and coached at every level of amateur hockey, has this to say about fitness: "The single most important ingredient of success in athletics or life is discipline. This means do what has to be done, when it has to be done, as well as it can be done, and do it that way all the time."

F I T

Stretching is a good way to prepare for games; it can help you avoid injuries and contribute to a healthy life. Even if your body is not flexible now, a stretching program will pay off in the future.

The idea is to be careful. Don't strain. As you become more flexible, stretch harder, hold the pose longer, or do more repeats.

A few simple stretching exercises

1. Sit on the floor. Put the soles of your feet together. Gently pull your feet toward you. (Try to bring your feet closer as you gradually loosen up over time.) Once your feet are as close as you can get them, gently lean forward to add tension. *Good for:* groin muscles, hamstrings (back of thigh).

Stretching

This exercise can prevent groin injuries—a common hockey hazard.

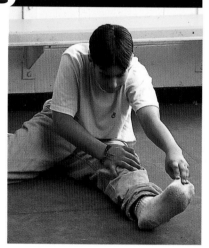

Good for both front and back of your legs. Being flexible pays dividends for life.

A good lower back stretch. That part of a hockey player's body takes a lot of hits.

2. Sit on the floor. One leg is stretched out in front of you; the other is folded back at your side. Gently lean back, stretching the front of your folded leg. Stop when you feel pressure on your knee. Now lean forward as far as you can, keeping your front leg flat. Hold this position as long as you feel is comfortable. Reverse legs and repeat. *Good for:* quadriceps (front of thigh) and hamstrings.
3. Sit on a chair. Cross one leg at the ankle over the knee of the other leg, keeping the calf horizontal. Lean forward. You should feel the strain in the buttock on the side of the crossed leg. Do this several times, then reverse legs. *Good for:* buttocks and lower back.

Weight training

If you are sure that you are finished growing, you are ready to lift weights. But weight training is hard on growing bodies—especially soft connective tissue, such as tendons and ligaments. Weights are also hazardous. Too much weight damages muscles.

Most kids do much of their growing between the ages of 12 and 16. So wait to do weights. There's plenty of time to get stronger. First, as a hockey player, you want to get better.

If you insist on adding zip to your shot, do push-ups and pull-ups. Do sets of five at first. Add sets as you get stronger. Push-ups and pull-ups are less dangerous because you are working with your own weight, which is more or less constant. As you are able to do more, you know you are becoming stronger.

Nutrition

The easiest way to improve your on-ice performance is to pay attention to what you eat. Eating well means eating a wide variety of foods; you need to eat from these four food groups every day:

- Dairy products
- Meat (including fish and poultry)
- Fruits and vegetables
- Breads, cereals and grains

Remember, playing hockey—including practice time, off-ice workouts and getting in shape for games—burns up 3,000–6,000 calories a day. That means you have to eat at least three main meals daily with second helpings, plus snacks between meals. You also need to drink lots of fluids, about eight glasses a day.

Your last chance to fuel up for a game is 24 hours before. Eat pastas, rice, breads and fruits to top up your blood sugar. These foods are your main source of energy. Three to four hours before the game is your last chance to eat without using up energy on digesting food. At this point, it is too late to get any jump from eating. But if you're hungry, have a light meal—maybe a light protein, such as tuna.

Swallow nothing but water in the last hour before game time. Most important, avoid sugared drinks and chocolate in that last hour, so that your energy doesn't take a nosedive from too much sugar. During the game, have two or three good swallows of water every 15 minutes.

T I P

For snacks, eat easy-to-digest foods, such as fruit. Skip the junk foods—potato chips, nachos, candy and French fries—they're fatty and too hard to digest.

Eat right

Photo credits

Photography by Stefan Schulhof/Schulhof Photography, except as indicated below:

Photos by Bruce Bennett Studios:
Front cover: Bruce Bennett
Back cover & title page spread (Paul Kariya), p. 8 (background), p. 9, p. 49: Art Foxall
Back cover & title page spread (Peter Forsberg, Wayne Gretzky), p. 1 (background), p. 7, p. 12, p. 14 (background), p. 15. p. 17, p. 25, p. 38, p. 78 (background), p. 79, p. 83: Bruce Bennett
Back cover & title page spread (Sergei Fedorov), p. 44 (background), p. 45: Mark Hicks
Back cover & title page spread (Ed Belfour), p. 30, p. 56 (background), p. 57, p. 61, p. 76: Claus Andersen
p. 18, p. 33, p. 59: Jim McIsaac
p. 21: Tony Biegun
p. 37, p. 54: Robert Laberge
p. 41: Michael Digirolamo
p. 46: John Giamundo
p. 69, p. 75: Richard Lewis

Photos by Kent Kallberg Studios: back cover & title page spread (Pavel Bure), p. 4, p. 88 (background), p. 89

Photos of Pat Quinn (pp. 3 & 5) and Ron Smith (p. 3) courtesy of the Vancouver Canucks